Neath & Port Talbot

Life

By David Roberts

www.bryngoldbooks.com

First published in Great Britain in 2011
by Bryngold Books Ltd.,
100 Brynau Wood, Cimla,
Neath, South Wales SA11 3YQ.

www.bryngoldbooks.com

Typesetting, layout,
editing and design
by Bryngold Books

ISBN 978-1-905900-23-7

Printed and bound
in Wales by
Gomer Press,
Llandysul, Ceredigion.

Contents

Appreciation

Neath & Port Talbot Life would not have been possible without the assistance of many people. Among them are my wife Cheryl, for her ceaseless support; Anthony Isaac, Neil Melbourne, John Vivian Hughes, John & Barbara Southard and Colin Scott who, once again, have all helped in so many different ways.

Then there are all those who have shared so many delightful photographs. Among them are Tony & Hilary Llewellyn, Brian Walters, Christine Meagher, Derry Moore, Dilys Jones, Elaine Wise, Robert Thomas, the late Eric Hill, Graham and Carol Gilbert, Steve and Kay Maclean, Margaret and Greg Herdman, Jeff Huckeridge, John and Jean Minshall, Robert Jones, the late Ken Kingdom, EJ Cross, John Newman, Roger and Veronica Gale, Mervyn and Betty Roberts, Steven H Jones, Bob & Ann Merchant, Val Thomas, Janice Austin, Ken Rees, Mike Hopkins, Eileen Cottey, Keith & Ann Davies, Steve Williams, VW Leyshon, Alan Pugsley, Alwyn Rees, Alun & Kay Rees, Anita Thomas, Anthony Prosser, Brenda Smith, TG Evans, Anne Brown, Peter Ryan, Vernon Smith, Will Hanford, Steve Dinham, John Jones, Lilian Thomas, Lindsey Evans, Lyndon Todd, Mary Gregory, Lynsey Sly, John Mathias, John Slater, Christine Basten, Brian Harry, Bill Adams, Mr & Mrs Les Hunt, Don Walters, Terry Jones, George Vincent , Steve Pitman, Angela Locke, Mrs D Jones, David Jones, Enid Farrell, John Matthews, Colin Walters, Helen Smith, Ken Evans, Port Talbot Library, the late Harry Humphries, Kester Reason, Anne Morgan, Carol Rainford, Mrs Parker, Rosemary Matthews, the late Morris Fish, Eunice Hunter Rowe, Brian Harry, Marie Hopkins, Malcolm & Mary Rees, Lucy King, Jean & Colin Griffiths, Allun Davies, Mrs Andrews, Mrs Thomas, Pamela Davies, Ruby Matthews, Viv & Susan Roberts, Chris Griffiths, Fred Harris, Steve & Lee Watkins, Mike Hoile, David Davies, Stan Thomas, Aileen Buckingham, the late Vincent Thomas, Chris & Paul Rowlands, Allen Morgans, Jenny Lewis and Mrs D Morris.

We are also grateful to those whose photographs may not have been selected for this book, purely on the grounds of space. Their part has been just as invaluable. Our thanks go to you all.

Share your photos

You too, can play a part in recording the history of your area by contributing photographs to the next Neath & Port Talbot nostalgia book. Please telephone 01639 643961 or e-mail david.roberts@bryngoldbooks.com to discover the ways in which you can do this. We would be delighted to hear from you. All photographs, black and white or colour, of people, places, events, streets, buildings, schooldays and sport are considered whatever their age, subject or format. They are all promptly returned. Also, if you have missed any of the previous 12 books then contact us now as some titles are still available. You can also check out our website at
www.bryngoldbooks.com
for details of our other fascinating local nostalgia books.

Foreword

As the First Citizen of the County Borough, I am privileged and delighted to have been asked to write a foreword for this edition and I would like to thank David for giving me this opportunity.

Like the many books from David Roberts before it, Neath and Port Talbot Life does what it says in the title and reflects much that has occurred in the two towns down through many decades.

Having previously gathered many thousands of images into what has evolved as an ever-growing album, David continues to amaze us by unearthing and sharing fresh photographs from the past. Each of these plays a part in preserving memories of our towns as they were and those who lived in them as they went about their daily lives.

Neath and Port Talbot Life offers us a unique comparison of today's towns against the way they once were and allows us to judge how change has slowly manifested itself.

What started as just one book for David, has now become 13 in consecutive years. This is something that few towns and cities across the length and breadth, not only of Wales, but the whole of Britain can boast. This new title and its predecessors serve as a unique, easily accessible, people's archive.

He will tell you that each of his books have only been possible through the willingness of ordinary, everyday people to contribute their own personal photographs. It is this as much as anything which sets the eagerly awaited publications apart and demonstrates the pride that is retained by the residents of our county borough.

Like the books before it Neath and Port Talbot Life shows us a plethora of aspects of all our lives, from street scenes to sport and school groups to transport, it is all here on these pages.

My own memory serves to remind me of how things were and how much has changed, but there are lots of occasions when a glance at a photograph, like the many in this book is enough to revive long-forgotten thoughts of people and places that were once familiar.

David has once again captured the spirit of the past. We applaud him for this and hope his efforts will continue long into the future. Sharing photographs through his books is a wonderful way in which we can all play a part in recording our history.

Neath and Port Talbot Life is something of which we can all be proud.

Councillor Harry Bebell,

Mayor of Neath Port Talbot,

September 2011.

United we stand

Neath and Port Talbot are two neighbouring, yet completely different, towns which have each made their own indelible impression on the world at large and continue to do so under a unified county borough banner.

Life in them these days is as fast-paced as anywhere else and while we all go about our daily lives, change can creep up on us, almost without warning. Often, it is only when delving into photographs drawn from down the decades that we can appreciate what has gone before. This, more than anything else becomes clear from looking at the many images gathered in Neath & Port Talbot Life.

Through the passage of time much has been written about the history of the towns from their humble beginnings. They have always retained a fierce individuality, something evident from the miscellany of images on the following pages. There is nothing wrong about that. Yet when times call for them to stand together, they do.

This book gives a flavour of the way the people in the two towns lived, worked and played and also how change affected them. What makes it different is the fact that like the books in this series that have gone before, most of the pictures have been shared by, and indeed were taken by, those same people themselves.

What that says, as another year has brought us both good news and bad, is that they have played a significant part in recording their own history. A history of which every single one of them can be proud.

David Roberts,
2011

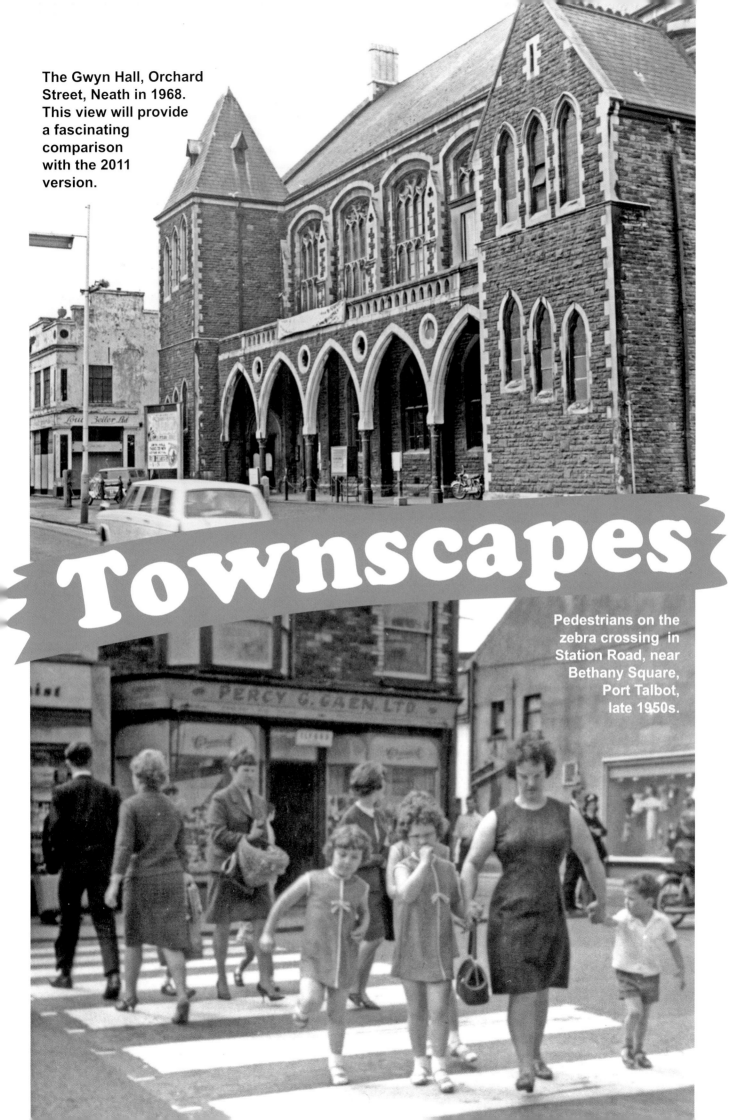

The Gwyn Hall, Orchard Street, Neath in 1968. This view will provide a fascinating comparison with the 2011 version.

Townscapes

Pedestrians on the zebra crossing in Station Road, near Bethany Square, Port Talbot, late 1950s.

Neath County School for Boys, Dwr-y-Felin Road, early 1900s.

With so little traffic in evidence, it is likely that this early 1950s view along Station Road, Port Talbot, was captured on a Sunday morning.

Looking across Aberavon towards the emerging Sandfields housing estate, and the beach mid-1950s.

New buildings erected in 1934 at Neath County School for Girls behind the original tennis court.

An atmospheric, late autumn afternoon view through the impressive wrought iron gateway of St Thomas Parish Church, Neath, 1959.

St Mary's Church, Aberavon, 1955. The houses behind are in St Mary's Place which were demolished to make way for the building of the town's inner by-pass.

Looking across Velindre and the former Trefelin Secondary School, from Tydraw Hill, Port Talbot, 1955.

One of the residents of Zoar Row shares a moment with his young son, 1952.

An aerial view of part of the raised section of the M4 at Velindre, Port Talbot, during construction, March 1965. The town's Drill Hall can be seen on the bottom left.

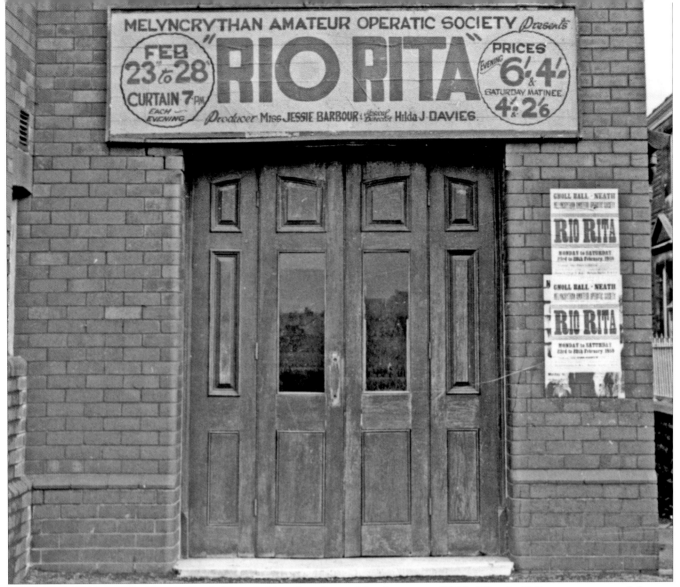

The Gnoll cinema at Gnoll Park Road, Neath, closed in January 1959. The building re-opened for one week from February 23-28, that year for the staging of Melyncrythan Amateur Operatic Society's successful production of the musical Rio Rita.

Oakwood Street, viewed from its junction with Tydraw Street, Port Talbot, mid-1960s.

The old, but still impressive town hall, Church Place, Neath, 1966.

A traffic warden directs vehicles at the junction of High Street and Water Street, Port Talbot prior to demolition of shops and streets to make way for town centre redevelopment, 1970.

The Royal Exchange public house at the junction of High Street and Cwmavon Road, Port Talbot, late 1969.

Ye Olde Grocerie Shoppe, London Road, Neath, 1976 served the locality for many years.

The bridge over the River Afan at High Street, Port Talbot, 1970. All of the buildings seen here vanished during town centre redevelopment.

The Bird in Hand public house, Water Street, Neath, late 1950s.

Wind Street, Neath, looking towards the Ancient Briton pub and telephone exchange in the distance, late 1960s. The buildings here were replaced by Tesco and later Wilkinsons.

Looking under the bridge that carried the main Swansea to Paddington railway line across Water Street, Aberavon, 1968.

The Mechanics Institute, Church Place, Neath with the Moose Hall and Duke of Wellington pub, visible in the background, 1968. This view was later obscured by the construction of flats.

The Water Street, Port Talbot, entrance to the town's Municipal Buildings and shopping arcade, 1969, shortly before town centre redevelopment.

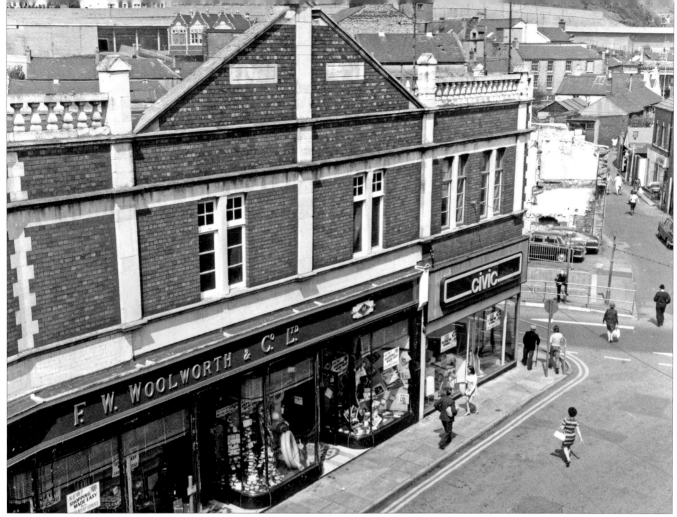

Port Talbot's original Woolworth's store at Church Street. It became known as the 'old' Woolworth's with the opening of a newer store in Station Road. Church Lane heads off to the right.

Library Road, Neath, after an overnight snowfall, February 1968.

Houses in London Road, Neath, after an overnight snowfall, February, 1969.

The first concrete beam is lowered into place for a new temporary road bridge for diverted traffic during Port Talbot town centre redevelopment, early 1970s. In the background, the former municipal buildings have yet to be demolished. The bridge now provides access for vehicles delivering to the Aberafan Shopping Centre's Wilkinsons store.

Clarence Street, Port Talbot, looking tired and run down, shortly before its demolition, 1971.

A low tide view across the River Neath westwards from The Quay, mid-1970s. The Tennant canal is the other side of the retaining wall.

The Majestic bingo club, previously the Odeon cinema, towers over these shops at Bethany Square, Port Talbot, early 1970s.

The rather dilapidated looking YMCA building at Orchard Street, Neath, early 1970s.

Looking up Eastland Road from Stockham's Corner, April 1972. The Butchers Arms public house, now The Highlander, is on the right.

Harwood's garage and filling station, Water Street, Aberavon, 1974.

Aberavon Post Office, Talbot Square, Port Talbot, 1972.

Looking along Windsor Road, Neath, towards Neath Methodist Church and
Stockham's Corner, April 1972.

Looking up from James Street towards St Thomas parish Church, Neath, August 1977. Bethlehem Green Calvinistic Methodist Church is on the left.

High Street, Port Talbot, looking west during excavation work linked to town centre redevelopment, 1974.

James Street Service Station, Neath, 1987.

Aberafan House, alongside the River Afan, Port Talbot, 1978.

An atmospheric view along one of the arcades at Aberafan Shopping Centre, leading out onto the riverside, 1980.

Work underway on the supports for Neath's northern link road bridge, 1987.

Thomas Street, Aberavon, after heavy snow, 1982.

Shops in Angel Street, Neath, 1987.

Roadworks underway during town centre development at Neath, 1988. This was the view up New Street towards the Square, with the Castle Hotel on the right.

Snow covered rooftops of houses in Abbey Road, Port Talbot, and surrounding streets, 1983.

Traffic queues in Eastland Road, Neath, August 23, 1988. The traffic flow was just one way then.

The impressive facade of Romilly Buildings, Talbot Road, Port Talbot, 1984.

Shops and offices at Talbot Road, near its junction with Abbey Road, Port Talbot, 1984.

Rows of concrete foundation piles between Angel Street and James Street, Neath mark the beginning of new retail development 1988.

Construction of what became Morrisons supermarket, on the site of James Street, 1988.

Shops in Station Road, Port Talbot, 1984.

Pedestrianisation work underway at Station Road, Port Talbot, late 1980s.

Crowds gather around the bandstand at Victoria Gardens, Neath, on a summer day, 1990.

Bring large bags and little money for the best bargains in Port Talbot was the message proclaimed across the front of the Jubilee Shopping Hall in Station Road, 1985. Originally a Fine Fare supermarket, it later became the town's Job Centre.

The Gnoll School just days before it was demolished in May 1993.

Stalls line Queen Street, Neath during a September Fair week, early 1990s.

Looking westwards across Port Talbot, 1985. The town's civic centre is in the foreground.

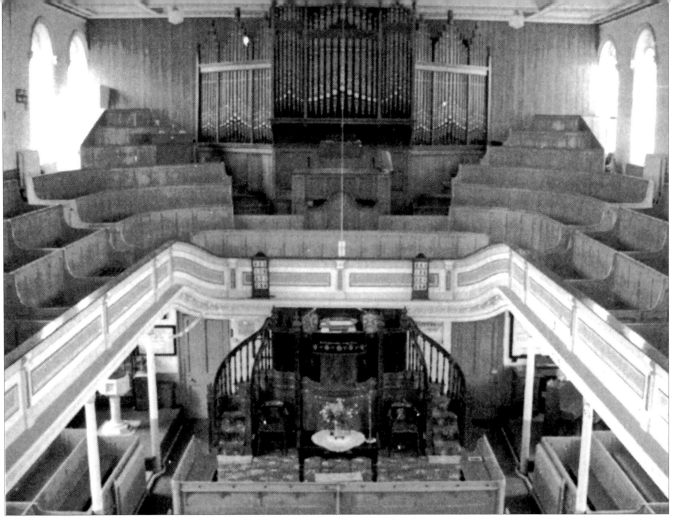

The pulpit and organ at Soar Maes-yr-Haf Chapel, Neath, 1994.

Looking into Forge Road, from Bethany Square, Port Talbot, during demolition of the Odeon Cinema, 1987.

A fascinating view across the waters of Port Talbot docks towards Aberafan House in the centre of the town, 1987. Beyond is the gateway to the Afan Valley.

Buildings at Neath Welsh School - Ysgol Gymraeg Castell Nedd - Woodland Road, Neath, 1990s.

Tanygroes Street, Port Talbot, late 1980s. The town's Royal Mail sorting office can be seen in the background.

The familiar names of Woolworths and Argos, present the retail face of Orchard Street, Neath, mid-1990s.

Once a hive of trading activity based around the long-time bakery from which it drew its name, Stockham's Corner presented a sad image shortly before its demolition in the late 1990s.

Demolition of Park House, Theodore Road, Port Talbot, 1988.

Looking east towards St David's Church, Neath from the roof of the town's multi-storey car park.

Trinity Methodist Church, Tydraw Street, Port Talbot, April 1993.

Carriageway widening and refurbishment work underway on the M4 eastbound, Pentyla off-slip, Port Talbot, 1991.

Victoria Gardens bus station, Neath, with two Town Mini buses up front, 1995.

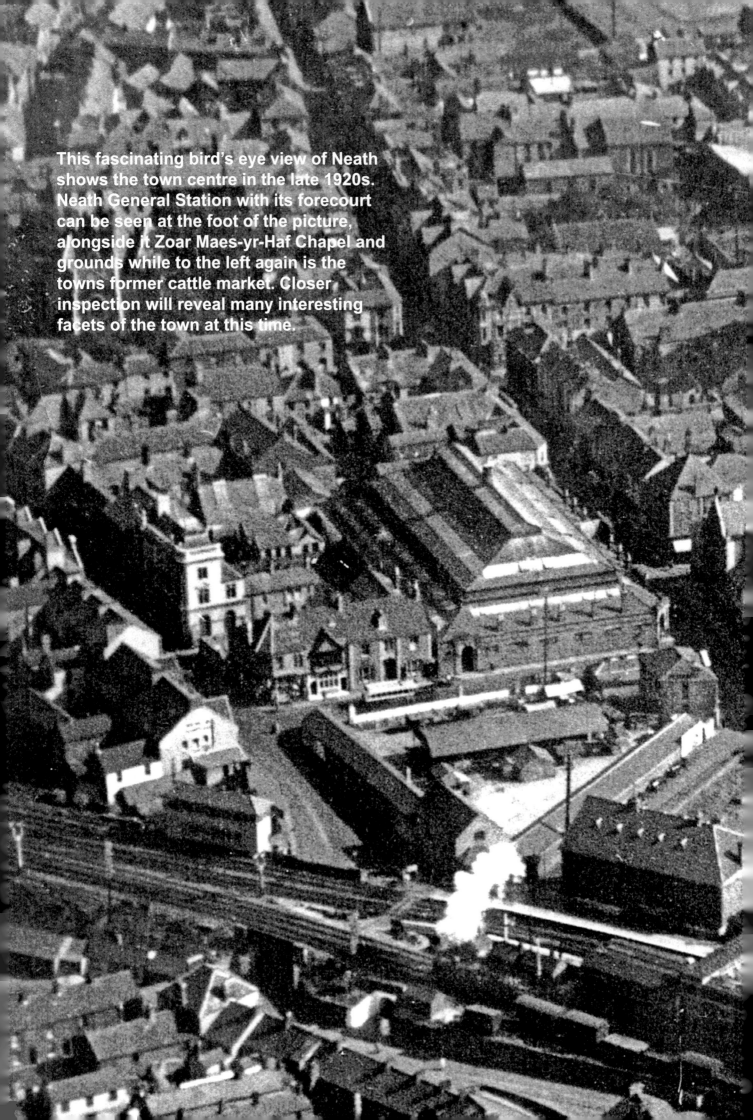

This fascinating bird's eye view of Neath shows the town centre in the late 1920s. Neath General Station with its forecourt can be seen at the foot of the picture, alongside it Zoar Maes-yr-Haf Chapel and grounds while to the left again is the towns former cattle market. Closer inspection will reveal many interesting facets of the town at this time.

Looking along Station Road, Port Talbot, towards the town centre, December 1993.

The former Blue Bell Inn, was known as Wallabies when this early 1990s photograph was taken. Both premises are now part of the Blue Bell hotel complex.

Demolition work underway of Neath Civic Centre, 2008.

This was the scene as a £35 million refurbishment of the Gwyn Hall, Orchard Street, Neath neared completion in 2007. The building was gutted by fire just months later before it could reopen.

Construction of the M4 between Pentyla and Baglan, Port Talbot, 1992.

Construction of the flyover which carries traffic off the M4 and towards Sunnycroft roundabout, Baglan, 1991.

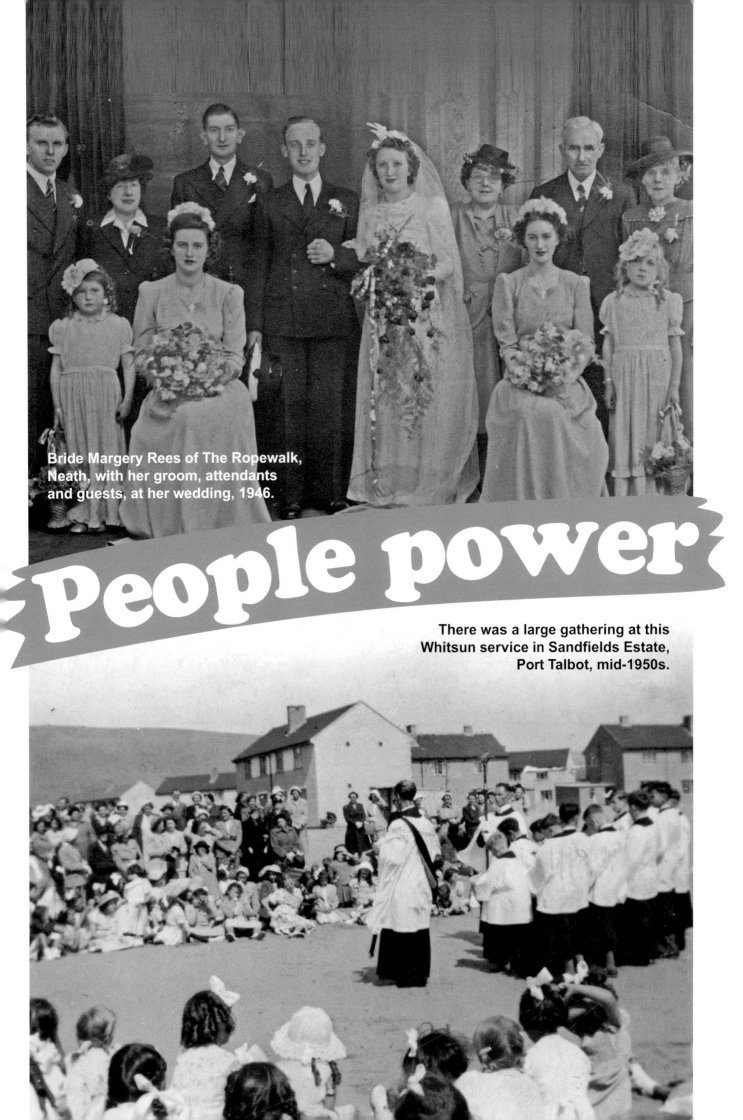

Bride Margery Rees of The Ropewalk, Neath, with her groom, attendants and guests, at her wedding, 1946.

People power

There was a large gathering at this Whitsun service in Sandfields Estate, Port Talbot, mid-1950s.

Betty Barwick and her family of Tonna, Neath, at her wedding, 1952. The reception was held at the village's Welfare Hall, now long demolished and replaced by a housing estate. The man wearing a hat is William Barwick, a well known figure in the village.

Members of Port Talbot Ex-servicemen's Club, 1926. With them is town Mayor, Hopkin Jones, himself a founder member and later president of the club. On the right of the Mayor is captain Andrew Talbot Fletcher, of Margam Castle, patron and the first president of the club. They are in the grounds of Ty Mawr, Talbot Square, now the town's civic square. The large building in the background is Aberavon Workingmen's Club, which opened in 1916.

These young women, gathered around a solitary clergyman, were members of a Port Talbot Sunday School group, 1914.

St. Anne's Church Choir, Tonna, Neath, 1947.

Members and organisers of
Rehoboth Band of Hope,
Briton Ferry, 1898.

These young boys all lived in Llewellyn Street, Aberavon, 1942.

Members of the congregation of St Paul's Church, Aberavon, at a bazaar they organised, 1962.

A group of Tonna teenagers with some girls they met during a holiday, 1952.

Members of the Llewellyn family of Angel Street, Aberavon, early 1930s.

These girls were all members of the St John Ambulance Brigade at Cwmavon. They were awarded the trophy for winning the Welsh First Aid Championships in 1971. Seen with them is Mayor of Port Talbot, Councillor Mel John and a branch officer.

Members of the Sunday School at Water Street Baptist Chapel, proudly display the shield they won in local scripture examinations, 1941.

The 3rd Neath Scout Troop during their attendance at the first Welsh Jamboree after the Second World War. It was held at Abergele, North Wales, 1947.

A gathering of Port Talbot Scouts and Cubs, with their divisional and district officers, early 1950s.

Members of the Sunday School at Ebenezer Baptist Chapel, Herbert Road, Melyncrythan, Neath. They are proudly displaying the shield they were awarded for winning the district Sunday School Union scripture exam in 1957.

The 14th Neath Cubs and Scouts with organisers, 1955.

A group of friends and neighbours from Cwmclais Road, Cwmavon, during a function at Antolin's Ros-a-Mar Rooms, Victoria Road, Aberavon, with the Mayoress of Port Talbot, Mrs Mary John also of Cwmclais Road, 1971. Her husband Mel was Mayor of the Borough of Port Talbot at the time.

Parents of members, with leaders of the 14th Neath Scout troop, 1955.

Long stay patients at Cymla Hospital, Neath, enjoy a moment of fun, 1958.

Mothers and children who lived in Lingfield Avenue, Sandfields, Port Talbot, 1972.

European youth exchange participants from Neath, Vienne, Udine and Esslingen at a function held at the home of Mr & Mrs Godwin, Briton Ferry, August 1963.

Just over 50 splendidly dressed teddy bears and their owners took part in a best dressed teddy competition held as part of childrens week at the Aberafan Shopping Centre, August 1979.

Members of the Sandfields Steppers walking group on a visit to Cardiff Castle, 2008.

Three youngsters from Illtyd Street, Llantwit, Neath, during celebrations of the Silver Jubilee of Queen Elizabeth II, 1977.

Prince Edward chats to Judith Watkins at Ysgol Hendre, Bryncoch, April 20, 2004. Judith was in charge of the community skills section of the Duke of Edinburgh Award scheme there.

A Christmas shopping event for disabled people at Woolworth's Orchard Street, Neath store with staff and representatives of the organisers, the Neath branch of The Red Cross, 1966.

Nurses from Neath General Hospital at a presentation ceremony at the Brangwyn Hall, Swansea where Prince Charles handed out their certificates, December 2, 1977.

A Sandfields, Port Talbot couple outside their prefab home, early 1950s. This was just one of the hundreds of similar temporary homes that were used to house residents. Meant to last for just 25 years many survived for far longer.

Around & About

Pausing for a break near Briton Ferry roundabout, looking towards the Church of Our Lady of the Assumption, mid-1960s.

One of the bridges over the Neath Canal at Giants Grave, Briton Ferry, early 1920s.

St Mary's Church, Aberavon, with houses in Richard Street in the background, 1873.

The school at Groes, Margam, 1910. It was demolished along with the village to make way for the M4 motorway.

The Swing Bridge over the River Neath, late 1930s. Built to carry the railway over the river it is one of the few in the UK to be built on a curve. It opened to allow for the passage of shipping.

The main street through Pantdu, Cwmavon, with the Oddfellows Arms on the right, 1910.

The surviving wing of Vernon House, Briton Ferry, 1950s. It was later demolished to make way for a housing development.

Looking north eastwards across Cimla Common towards construction of some of the first new homes on the Glannant Estate, early 1960s. Glannant Farm is just visible in the distance.

Bridges and viaducts seem to have existed in profusion in Pontrhydyfen, when this 1920s photograph was taken.

Tonna Primary School, Neath, April 26, 1994. The building was eventually demolished to be replaced by Noddfa Newydd Chapel.

Station Road, Crynant, on a wet winter's afternoon, 1995.

Construction of Neath river bridge at Briton Ferry, early 1950s. Started in 1949, this was the UK's biggest civil engineering project since the end of the Second World War and wasn't finished until the autumn of 1955. Today it is dwarfed by the M4 river crossing.

This was the new Council School at Cwmavon, shortly after it was opened in the 1920s.

The ruins of Neath Abbey, with a bridge over the Tennant Canal alongside, 1950.

Looking across Victoria Road, from the sand dunes at Little Warren, towards Sandfields prefabs that housed some of the town's residents for many years, late 1940s.

A church service is conducted from the ornate bandstand at Memorial Park, Taibach, Port Talbot, late 1940s.

The foundations of a bungalow being built in Butlers Field, Cimla Common, Neath, 1952. It was one of the first privately built properties in the town after the Second World War. The imposing frontage of Crynallt House can be seen in the background.

Margam Abbey, castle, Orangery and surrounding cottages, with the lake just visible on the left, 1948.

Burned out cottages in the Cwm, Baglan, near Baglan Church, 1950s.

The pulpit and interior of Ebenezer Chapel, Herbert Road, Melyncrythan, Neath, early 1970s.

Petrol was far cheaper in the final days of this filling station on the old Neath Valley trunk road at Aberdulais. The picture was taken on April 26, 1994. Along with neighbouring properties it was later demolished to make way for the new dual carriageway.

Colliery railway sidings full of coal wagons in the Goytre Valley, 1950s.

Eglwys Nunydd farmhouse, Water Street, Margam, in 1951 and as it is today. The building fell into a state of disrepair before undergoing a lengthy restoration project guided by Francis and Patricia Needs. The other pictures show the farmhouse in its dilapidated state and also the fireplace in the original kitchen.

A construction project underway on the seafront at Aberavon, early 1960s, The crowds in front of the scaffolding appear to be at the start of one of the marathons that started and finished here.

The Branch bridge at Abergarwed, Resolven, 1966. It was later washed away in floods.

An aerial view of the BP Baglan Bay chemical plant during the early 1990s. Construction of the M4 missing link can be seen at the top right.

Cascades at the Gnoll Country Park, Neath 1984.

The main
entrance
to the former
Aberavon
gas works at
Victoria Road,
June 1989.

The A465 flyover at Neath Abbey with
Drummau Mountain behind, 1980.

The library at Taibach,
Port Talbot, July, 1988.
The building was
opened in 1917 as the
Carnegie Free Library.

This fascinating figure appeared on the blackened mountainside overlooking Port Talbot during 2003. Created from hundreds of bags of flour it was reputed to be a salute to the efforts of the firemen who had fought the flames on Mynydd Dinas.

Construction work underway on bungalows at The Meadows, Cimla, Neath, 1988.

Emily Thomas outside her shop which stood next to the Bowen Arms public house, Skewen, 1930s.

Off to the shops

Clothiers W Gibbon & Co, were convinced that their shop in Station Road, Port Talbot, offered the cheapest clothing in Wales in 1903.

Proprietor Herbert Harrison
outside his Neath shop, 1905.

The Central Pharmacy chemist shop
run by G D Loveluck in Station Road,
Port Talbot, early 1900s.

Shops in New Street, Neath,1910. Today, the Next clothing store is opposite.

Staff outside the Briton Ferry & District Co-operative Society's, Melyncrythan butchery shop, early 1930s. It certainly appears to have been a well-stocked establishment.

The South Wales Tea and Provisions Merchants' store at High Street, Aberavon would no doubt have been popular with the town's shoppers in 1903. Proprietor J Waite described the business as the up-to-date family grocers selling rich fragrant teas and freshly ground coffees.

Everything for the budding photographer and specialist alike was available from the Burgess drug and photographic stores at 45 & 47 High Street, Aberavon, in 1903.

Two women on a shopping trip to Neath, 1949. They are seen in a bustling Green Street.

Staff of the grocery store of the Briton Ferry & Neath Co-operative Society at Neath Road, Briton Ferry, late 1950s.

The Co-operative store, Resolven, early 1950s. Its well-stocked windows indicate that it catered for many different needs of the village.

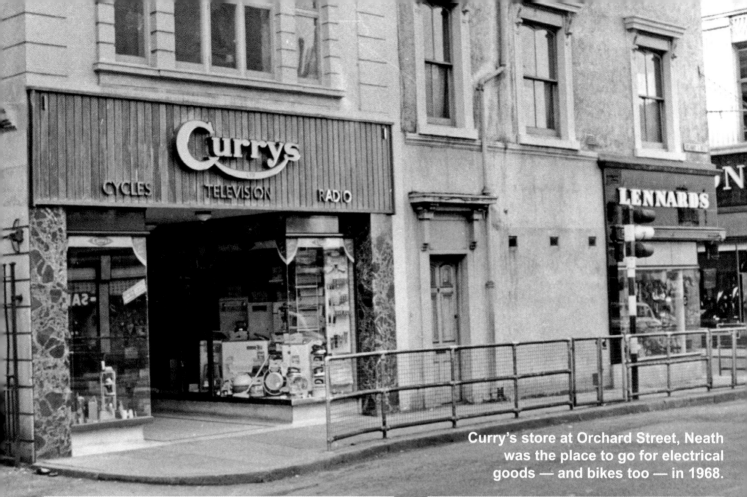

Curry's store at Orchard Street, Neath was the place to go for electrical goods — and bikes too — in 1968.

This was how the Cigar Depot run by J A Thomas displayed its wares to passers by in Station Road, Port Talbot, in the early 1900s.

Parties were catered for, to any number and in the best style, at Comley's family hotel and restaurant, Station Road, Port Talbot, in the early 1900s.

Harry Amyes, his wife and daughter Eunice in The Wood Shop, Skewen, which they opened and ran for many years, 1958.

Shops at Commercial Road, Taibach, early 1970s.

Models in a fashion parade held at the Gwyn Hall, Neath by the Briton Ferry & Neath Co-operative Society, August 1966. A local newspaper report at the time said the parade offered something for everyone's taste. The attractive models are Mai Morgan, Jeanne Goodwin, Marian White, Margaret Adams and Enid Davies.

A popular sweet stall at Neath Market where Pic 'n' Mix was 50p a quarter, in the mid-1990s!

Retail premises in Commercial Road, Taibach, Port Talbot, late 1980s.

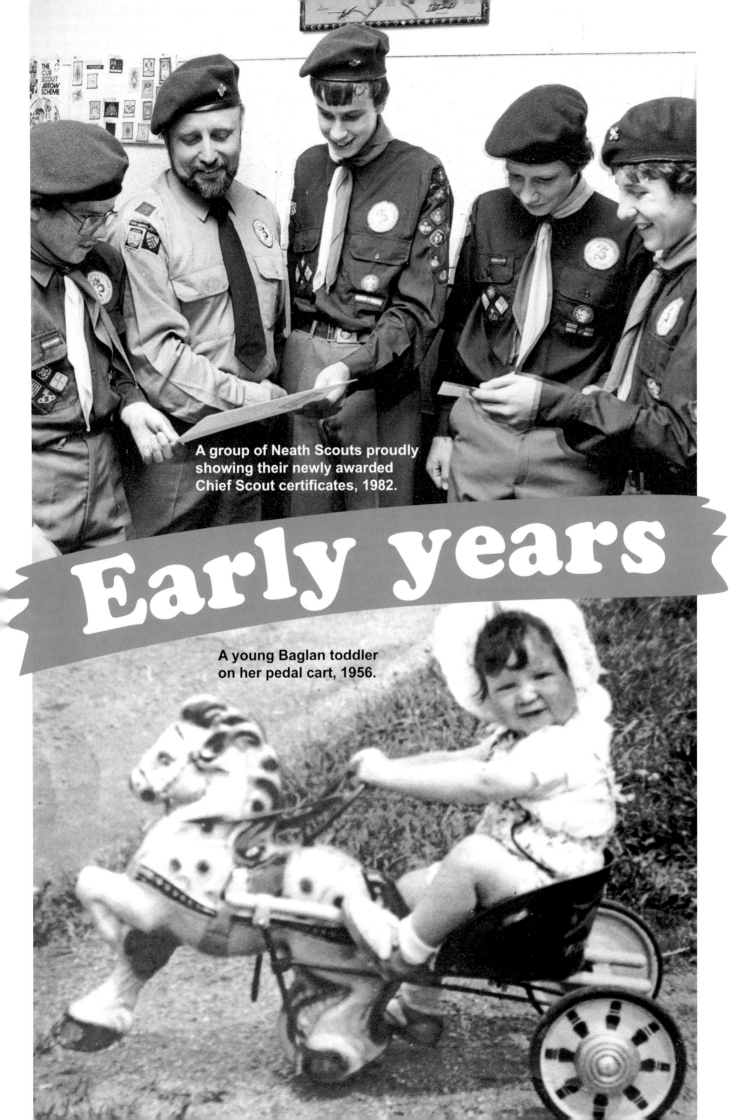

A group of Neath Scouts proudly showing their newly awarded Chief Scout certificates, 1982.

Early years

A young Baglan toddler on her pedal cart, 1956.

These three youngsters lived in cottages on Penycae Road, Port Talbot, 1926.

Sunday best for the photographer! The three eldest of six children of the Williams family who lived at Charles Street, Aberavon, 1929.

Young boys enjoy a game of marbles at Tonna, Neath, late 1940s.

Children enjoy a spin on the roundabout at the playground in the Gnoll Grounds, now the Gnoll Country Park, Neath, mid-1950s.

A father and his young son and daughter walk through fields at Baglan, 1964.
The M4 motorway now runs through this spot on the seaward side of Pinetree Car Sales.

Neath Cubs and their leaders proudly stand to attention in front of the band stand, Victoria Gardens, Neath, 1981.

Children of members of Port Talbot and District Amateur Operatic Society with Father Christmas at a festive party in the mid-1970s.

Winners of the Western Mail children's art competition with some of their work, at Sandfields library, Port Talbot, 1974. Their teacher and the Mayor of Port Talbot, Councillor Edith Letts look on.

Members of the 8th Neath (Crynant) Cub Scouts on a visit to Horton Inshore Lifeboat station, Gower, 1992.

A group of children enjoy a birthday party at the Wimpy Bar, The Parade, Neath, 1988.

Members of the 1st and 2nd Port Talbot Boys' Brigade Companies at Aberavon Beach for the local inter-group games, 1978.

The 5th Port Talbot (St Theodore's) Scout troop at the Welsh Jamboree, Gredinton, Wrexham, 1981.

Two young girls in the lane behind their home at Osterley Street, Briton Ferry, mid-1950s.

Members of Neath Air Training Corps during their summer camp at RAF Lyneham, Wiltshire, 1984.

Members of the 2nd Baglan Brownie Pack on church parade, 1984.

The chorus line from a musical staged by Port Talbot Amateur Operatic Society, mid-1920s.

Music & dance

Singer Allun Davies with members of Catwg Children's Choir who took part in a variety concert he organised, 1966.

Members of the Brython Minstrel Group, of Briton Ferry, 1917.

Members of the Queen
Mary Stewards jazz
band, Cwmavon, 1935.

Port Talbot Town Band outside Ty Mawr, the big house that stood near Talbot Square, early 1930s.

Members of the amateur theatrical society that flourished at the Oil Refinery, Llandarcy, during a dress rehearsal for their production of Abdul Karim, 1929.

Pupils of Cimla Infants School at their Christmas concert, 1954.

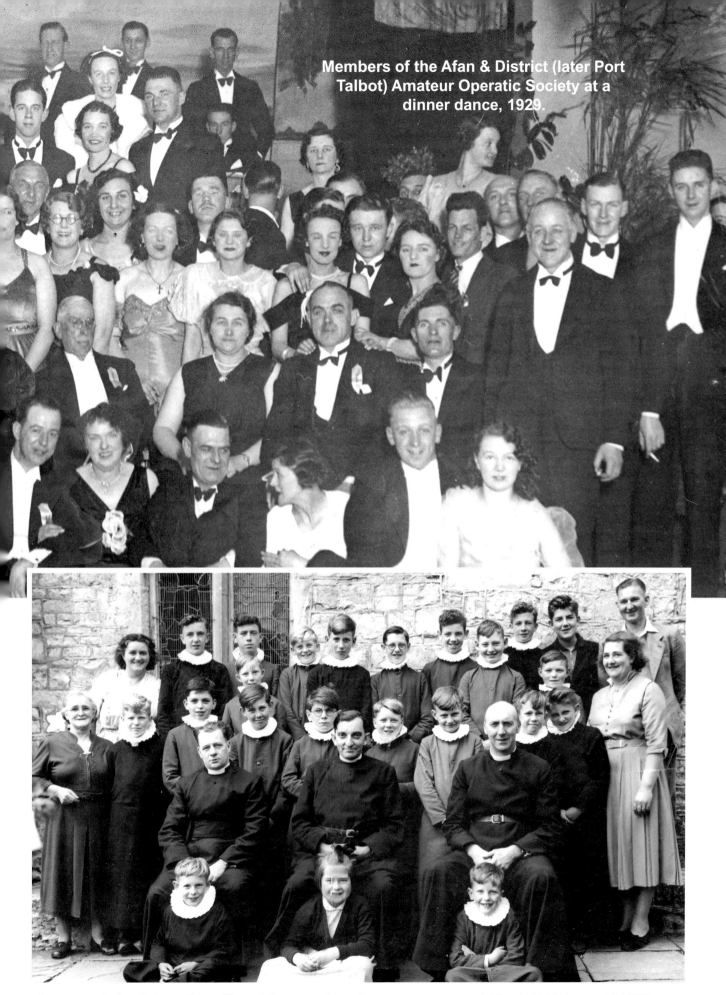

Members of the Afan & District (later Port Talbot) Amateur Operatic Society at a dinner dance, 1929.

A group of choristers, from three Skewen churches, on a course at Llantwit Major, mid 1950s.

St Paul's Church Choir, Aberavon, with curate, Rev Maundy Phillips and congregation members 1935.

This jazz band was known as the Cwmafan Coons in the early 1950s.

Participants in the Nativity production by pupils of Cimla Infants School, 1956. It was staged in the small chapel that stood on the nearby common.

Eric and Valerie Rees during a performance of The Desert Song by Melyncrythan Amateur Operatic Society, 1967.

The chorus line of a Melyncrythan Amateur Operatic Society production, late 1950s.

Members of Neath Amateur Operatic Society who took part in its successful production of The Merry Widow, 1959.

The original and popular Margam Saints music group, in full swing, late 1950.

The choir of St Paul's Church, Aberavon, during celebrations to mark its 50th anniversary, 1961.
In the centre of the group is the Rev Glyn Simon, who later became Archbishop of Wales.

The chorus line of Melyncrythan Amateur Operatic Society's production of South Pacific, 1962.

Some of those who took part in Melyncrythan Amateur Operatic Society's production of
The Desert Song, 1967.

The cast of a production by Briton Ferry Amateur Operatic Society, 1960s.

The female chorus of Port Talbot and District Amateur Operatic Society when they took part in the Margam Festival, 1981.

A chorus group from Melyncrythan Amateur Operatic Society's production of Showboat, 1965.

The Baptist Women's League choir with women from Orchard Place Baptist Church, Neath, mid-1960s.

Members of the Girls' Brigade at Taibach Wesley Methodist Church with the shield they were awarded for winning a competition at the 1967 National Eisteddfod held at Bala.

A scene from one of the successful Passion Plays staged at Margam Park during the 1980s.

Members of Cadoxton Opera Group at the Gwyn Hall, Neath during a performance of Nabucco, 1983.

Participants in a Scout and Guide gang show at the Gwyn Hall, Orchard Street, Neath 1994.

St Paul's Church Choir, Aberavon, 1998.

A scene from the Melyncrythan Amateur Operatic Society production of the hit show,
A Funny Thing Happened On The Way To The Forum, early 1970s.

Pupils at Groes Primary School, Bertha Road, Margam, Port Talbot, shortly after its official opening, July 10, 1973.

Lesson time

Pupils at Bryncoch Church in Wales Primary School, with their teacher, 1967.

Class 5 pupils with their teacher at Neath Road School, Briton Ferry, early 1900s.

A class at Central Girls Junior School, Port Talbot, 1930.

Pupils of Standard II, Eastern Boys School, Taibach, Port Talbot, 1927.

Miss Kitty Thomas's Sunday School class at Orchard Place Baptist Chapel, Neath, winners for the third time, of the coveted Missionary Shield, June 23, 1936.

Pupils at Eastern Primary School, May 1962. Barry Kirk, alias Captain Beaney is seated second left.

Pupils at Tywyn Infants School, Sandfields, Port Talbot, on St David's Day, 1959.

Gnoll Girls Secondary School pupils on a trip to Ogmore Youth Camp, 1952.

Class 6A Sandfields Primary School, Pendarvis Terrace, Aberavon, 1946.

A class at Melyn Boys' Junior School, Neath, with their teacher 1952.

Some of the pupils who attended Neath Girls Grammar School, 1965.

Pupils of Central School, Port Talbot, December 1955.

Girls of Crynallt Infants School, Cimla, Neath, St David's Day, 1986.

A Class at Catwg Primary School, Cadoxton, Neath, 1973.

Form 2L, Sandfields Comprehensive School, Port Talbot, summer 1962.

Miss Shanahan's class, 3B at St Joseph's Junior School, Port Talbot, 1954.

St David's Day celebrations at Melyn Nursery School, Neath, 1975.

A social studies class at Dyffryn Comprehensive School, Margam, Port Talbot, with the town's Mayor, Councillor Mrs May Charles, 1968.

Pupils of class 5 Gnoll Infants School, Neath, 1979.

Youngsters at Gnoll Junior School, Neath, dressed in traditional Welsh costume to celebrate St David's Day, 1978.

A class of pupils at Glanafan Comprehensive School, Port Talbot, 1978.

A class at Crynallt Infants School, Cimla, Neath, 1978.

Class 2, Central Junior School, Port Talbot, 1979.

Pupils at Dyffryn Comprehensive School, Port Talbot, with their teacher, Mrs G Bowen, 1983.

Pupils of form 1E Crynallt Junior School, Cimla, Neath, with their teacher, 1979.

The nursery class at Eastern Primary School, Taibach, Port Talbot, 1985.

A group of year 10 pupils at Dwr-y-felin Comprehensive School, Neath, 1980.

Form 1M, Cefn Saeson Comprehensive School, Cimla, Neath with their teacher, 1979.

Pupils of form 5U, Glanafan Comprehensive School, Port Talbot, 1986.

Pupils at Sandfields Infants School, Port Talbot, St David's Day, 1987.

Class J3, Alderman Davies Church in Wales School, Neath, with teacher Sandra Knight, 1989.

The iron ore carrier Hoegh Rainbow is eased into her berth at Port Talbot Tidal Harbour by two tugs, early 1970s.

Moving ways

A group of motorcycle enthusiasts at Neath Abbey ruins, 1923.

The first coach operated by Ken Hopkins Coaches Tonna, late 1949.

Two Western Welsh Omnibus Company employees with an AEC Regal vehicle at the company's Cadoxton Road, Neath depot, mid-1930s.

The SS Amazon, wrecked on Margam Sands during a severe gale with loss of all lives, 1908.

A Harley Davidson motorcycle takes part in time trials at Pontrhydyfen, 1929. Visible in the background is the aqueduct built in 1825. It supplied water to the wheel which generated the blast for the Pontrhydyfen Ironworks. The watercourse was 4 feet wide and 3 ft deep and flanked by footpaths either side. The structure is 495 ft long, 75 ft high and 13ft wide, with four arches. Behind that can be seen the arches that carried the South Wales Railway.

Vessels displaying a mix of sail and steam power present a busy picture of Port Talbot Docks, early 1900s.

The SS Brodland which came to grief at Port Talbot, 1913.

A coal train heads through Resolven station on August 30, 1962.

A local passenger train hauled by locomotive 6673 at Resolven station on August 30, 1962.

A pleasure boat languishes in the low-tide mud of the River Neath in the shadow of the road bridge mid-1960s.

A 1939 Hillman Convertible and a Morris Minor with one of their proud owners, Doll Adams, at Cimla Common, 1959.

FBP 986

Brothers Keith and Brian Walters alongside a Standard car they had been repairing outside their home in Bowen Street, Melyncrythan, Neath, 1958.

Cyril Samuel with his car in front of Cwmavon Brickworks, Port Talbot, 1950.

A mixed freight train at
Neath on July 27, 1963.
The locomotive is
Number 48438.

Locomotive 3798 waits its next
turn of duty in the parcels yard
that stood at the back of Neath
station, September 14, 1963.

Pit ponies that hauled drams at Goytre Colliery, Port Talbot are given an airing and some exercise
by two local lads, mid-1950s.

A typical daily scene at Neath General railway station, February 29, 1964.

Clearing spoil tips at Cwmavon with Tabor Chapel in the background in the 1960s. The chapel was demolished in 1977.

A tight squeeze as a tug gently guides a vessel into the lock at Port Talbot Docks, late 1960s.

Crowds flock to view this Castle Class steam special when it stopped at Neath, 1985.

The canal barge Enfys on the Neath Canal, at Resolven, mid-1990s.

Rows of coal trucks and mineral wagons lined up at Port Talbot docks waiting to transfer their cargo to vessels that would carry it on the next ocean-going stage of its journey, early 1950s.

A pair of steam tugs guide a cargo vessel to her berth in Port Talbot docks, early 1960s.

Port Talbot docks was one of many around the country that became increasingly congested as ships were brought to a standstill during a strike by members of the National Union of Seamen, May 1966.

An air ambulance which landed on Cimla Common to pick up an injured person, 2007.

Tugs shepherd a crane barge involved in construction of Port Talbot Deep Water Harbour, late 1960s.

Cargo being transferred from lorries to a vessel at Port Talbot Docks, mid-1960s.

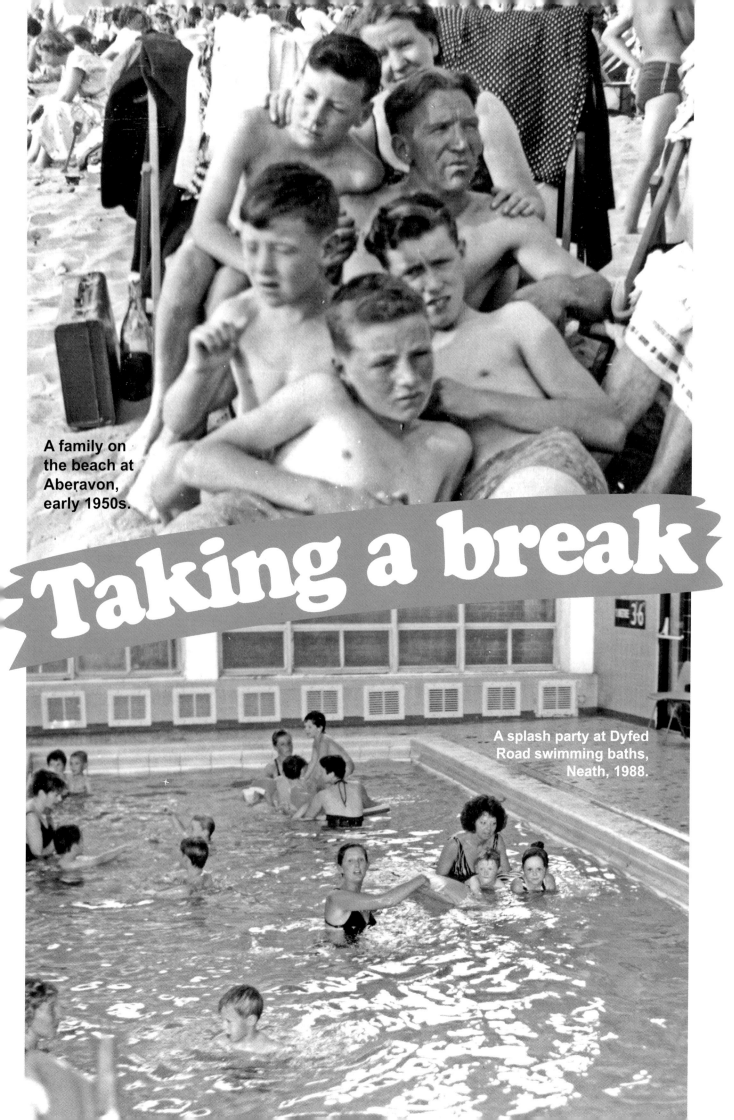

A family on the beach at Aberavon, early 1950s.

Taking a break

A splash party at Dyfed Road swimming baths, Neath, 1988.

Employees of the Port Talbot Dry Dock Company during their annual works outing, mid-1930s.

Employees of the Prudential Insurance Company's Neath office at Bristol on a day out, 1933.

Briton Ferry residents pose for one for the album on a trip to Blackpool, 1953.

Tonmawr residents on a trip to Blackpool, early 1950s.

Residents of Talbot Road, Westernmoor, Neath, on a Sunday outing to Rotherslade Bay, Gower, 1955.

A group of girls on a litter-strewn Aberavon Beach, 1937.

A Baglan family on holiday at Butlins holiday camp, Pwllheli, August 1953.

A group of Port Talbot lads on holiday at Butlins, Pwllheli, 1957.

Regulars of the Cross Keys pub, Dock Street, Briton Ferry, ready to set off on a day trip aboard a chartered N&C luxury coach, late 1960s.

Young people from Orchard Place Baptist Church, Neath were among this gathering at a summer school in Boscombe, 1961.

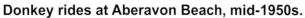

Crowds throng Aberavon Beach on a mid-summer day, mid-1960s.

Donkey rides at Aberavon Beach, mid-1950s.

A group of Metal Box employees and their families on a trip to Blackpool, mid-1960s.

Giving three ice cream cones a licking seems to have been the way to cool off after a visit to the fairground at Aberavon Beach, late 1970s.

Three likely lads from Taibach, Port Talbot, complete with giant bottle of Mackeson stout, enjoy a trip to Blackpool, mid-1960s.

Two Tonna Beavers enjoying a trip to Gunsmoke, the Wild West town at Seven Sisters Sawmills, 1990.

A group of lads from Neath and Briton Ferry on a holiday at Butlins 1962.

Pupils from Sandfields Comprehensive School, Port Talbot, with their teacher, Mr G Williams, on a day trip to Tenby, 1960.

The mother, right, of long time Briton Ferry cobbler John Melbourne, her daughter and sister, all set for a day trip to Carmarthenshire in a fine looking saloon car, late 1930s.

Sunseekers line the steps in front of the promenade at Aberavon Beach, summer 1961.

Great Western Railway staff at Resolven station, 1910.

Hard at work

Dockers unloading pit props at Port Talbot Docks, late 1950s.

Employees at the Steel Company of Wales, Port Talbot, 1952.

The signalman and a group of railwaymen at Neath East signal Box, 1940s.

Workers at Onllwyn Colliery Washery, 1939.

Librarians at work in Port Talbot central library, 1966.

Two Neath men with china chamber pots they were selling at Neath's September Fair, late 1940s.

Janice Hall and Anita Bailey who worked at Boots the Chemist, Wind Street, Neath, 1957.

Stowing steel coils in the hold of a ship at Port Talbot Docks, early 1960s.

Neath and District Post Office Home Guard detachment, 1942.

A careful hand signal to the crane operator and another boulder is laid in the correct position during the construction of Port Talbot's Deep Water Harbour, 1968.

Women workers on the lines at Neath Sheet Steel and Galvanising Works, early 1950s.

Two women workers at the Metal Box factory, Neath, Christmas time early 1950s.

Some of the women who worked at the Morris Cohen underwear factory, Purcell Avenue, Sandfields, Port Talbot, during the mid-1960s.

Port Talbot Borough Council employees on one of two double deck buses the authority bought from South Wales Transport and converted into travelling workshops. They are in the mess section which was on the upper deck, 1971.

Men and machines at work in the hold of a giant iron ore carrier discharging its cargo at Port Talbot Deep Water Harbour, 1972.

Rheola Aluminium Works, near Resolven, Neath Valley, early 1960s.

Dockers stowing tinplate in the hold of a cargo vessel berthed at Port Talbot Docks, mid-1960s.

Representatives of Neath's Magistrates, Press, the legal profession and Police, 1950.

Members of the typing pool together with secretaries at BP Baglan Bay celebrating the wedding of
The Prince of Wales and Lady Diana, July 28th, 1981.

The first group of locally trained foremen at Ford's Jersey Marine plant receiving their certificates
from the plant's manager, Frank Welton, 1969.

Retained firemen in front of one of the appliances at Neath fire station, Cimla, early 1980s.

Groundsmen and gardeners take a break from their labours in Vivian Park, Aberavon, amidst a massive bed of tulips, mid-1980s.

Post office staff from Neath, Port Talbot and Swansea proudly display the 30 year long service awards they received during a special presentation ceremony, 1991.

A group of Port Talbot fireman in their rescue kit, mid-1980s.

The No 4 blast furnace crew at Corus steelworks, Port Talbot, October 4, 1997.

Staff of the customer care department at Colour Care photo processing laboratory, Neath Abbey Industrial Estate, Neath, late 1980s.

Workmen at the Baglan Foundry company, Melyncrythan, Neath, 1981.

A number of Neath and Port Talbot firemen are included in this picture taken at Newtown Fire Station, Powys, at a 20 year, long service presentation ceremony, 2000. The group includes an array of senior fire service personnel and no fewer than three Lords Lieutenant of the counties served by the brigade at that time.

The fairy queen and her attendants from Kingdon Owen Road, Neath, during celebrations to mark the Coronation of Queen Elizabeth II, June 1953.

Let's celebrate

Children at Goytre, Port Talbot during their Whitsun procession, 1949.

Members of Neath Mission in the town's Windsor Road, during the annual Whitsun procession, 1949.

Residents and children of Saltoun Street, Margam, Port Talbot hold a street party to celebrate the Festival of Britain, 1951.

The newly crowned Aberafan May Queen with attendants and event organisers, early 1950s.

Employees of Resolven and District Co-operative Society and their guests during a Christmas party, early 1950s.

Staff of Chidzoy's fruiterers, Station Road, Port Talbot, during a Christmas night out, mid-1950s.

Part of a procession at Briton Ferry Road, Neath, 1949. The shops behind them were demolished in the spring of 2011.

Wearing ceremonial headgear, a contingent
of firemen marches down Station Road, Port
Talbot, possibly during a parade to mark the
Silver Jubilee of King George V, 1935.

Pupils of Melyn Boys School, Neath, all dressed up for their annual Christmas party, 1952.

Members of the congregation of Ebenezer Chapel, Herbert Road, in Gnoll Park Road, Neath, during the town's Whitsun procession, early 1950s.

Smartly dressed participants in a Whitsun procession in Port Talbot, 1951.

Residents of a Sandfields street at their Festival of Britain party, 1951.

Staff of BP Refinery, Llandarcy, at one of the popular dinner dances they held at the Brangwyn Hall in the 1960s.

Children at a Festival of Britain street party at the back of Margam Terrace, Port Talbot, 1951.

One of the floats in Cimla Rugby Club's carnival, 1969.

A well attended civic parade proceeds along Orchard Street, Neath, June 1968.

Church and chapelgoers from Aberavon and Port Talbot gather in the Square for their Whitsun procession through the town, early 1950s.

Two young residents of Florence Street, Neath, Fred Harris and his cousin Janice Griffiths, in fancy dress to celebrate the Coronation of Queen Elizabeth II, 1953.

Representatives of Port Talbot Salvation Army Corps lay a wreath at the cenotaph on Armistice Day, early 1950s.

Members of the congregation, young and old, of Holy Cross Church, Port Talbot, prepare to take part in a Whitsun procession, 1955.

Residents of Cove Road, Sandfields, Port Talbot, tuck in to some tasty food and drink at the party they held to celebrate the Festival of Britain, 1951.

Rev Clifford Thomas and his wife, Grace, together with members of Orchard Place Baptist Church Senior Guild, during celebrations to mark its 21st anniversary,1972.

Employees of the wages department at the Distillers Company Ltd, carbide works, Margam, at their Christmas dinner, 1964.

Members of the Mother's Union of St Paul's Church, Aberavon, marching along Castle Street, during the 1960s.

Tonna Cubs, all dressed up as a pack of cards, for the village's carnival, 1988.

Cimla Promenaders jazz band on parade at Cimla Common, 1984.

A street party to celebrate the Silver Jubilee of Queen Elizabeth II at Pine Valley estate, Cwmavon. 1977.

These youngsters were dressed up as dustbin men during a carnival at Baglan, mid-1960s.

Members of the Aberdulais branch of the Royal British Legion take part in an
Armistice Day parade, 1981.

Ynysfach Primary School netball team, Resolven, 1982.

Team spirit

Members of the Welsh rugby squad during a training session on Aberavon Beach, prior to the All Blacks Tour, 1969.

The Neath RFC team and officials, 1906-07.

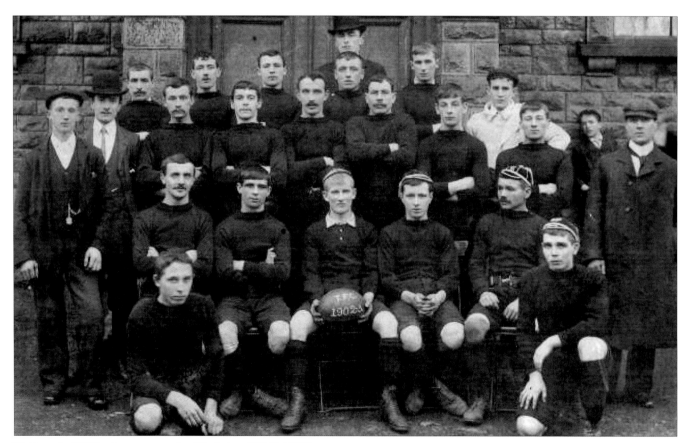

Taibach RFC players and officials, 1902-1903.

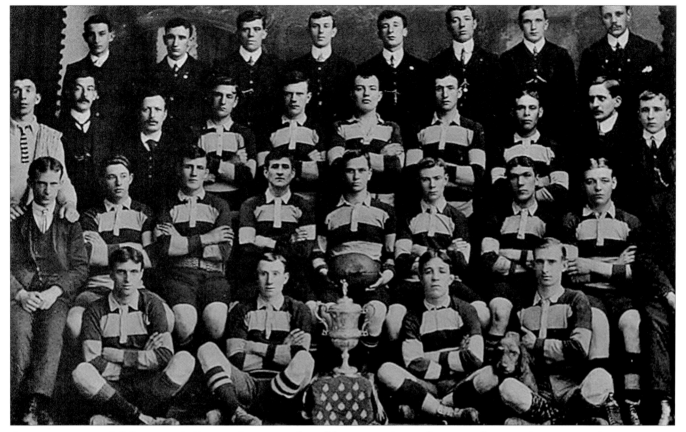

St Theodore's RFC, Port Talbot, who were local league champions and cup winners, 1910-11.

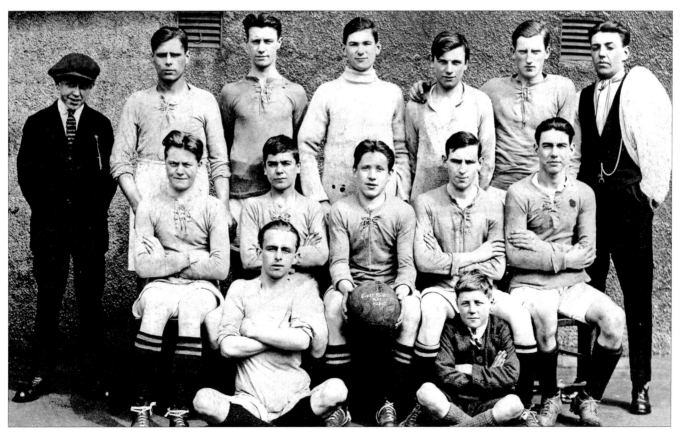

The football team at Cwrt Sart School, 1920.

An Aberavon RFC team of the late 1930s.

Nine members of a football team at Briton Ferry, mid-1930s.

Neath Harlequins RFC with the spoils of a successful season, 1930s.

Eastern School rugby squad, Taibach, with their teacher and headteacher, 1947-1948.

Briton Ferry Boys Club members, with some of the club stalwarts,1930s.

One of Taibach RFC's successful 1960s teams.

The under 15s rugby team at Glanafan Grammar School, Port Talbot, 1960-1961.

Briton Ferry bowls team members and officials, mid-1930s.

Members of the Neath GPO cricket team and officials, 1938.

Scouts who took part in a sports day at Traethmelyn School, Sandfields, Port Talbot, late 1960s.

The judo team of Aberavon Boys' Club at a Scout's Field Day, Kenfig, 1965.

Members and officials of Briton Ferry Bowls Club, late 1940s.

Members of the Neath Schoolboys Cricket XI who were beaten by Cardiff in the final of the Western Mail Shield competition at the Gnoll Ground, Neath, on Friday, July 14, 1950.

The relay team of Fleming House at Sandfields Comprehensive School, Port Talbot, winners of the event in the school's annual sports day, 1969.

A group of Port Talbot anglers proudly display some of their spoils from a day's fishing during a trip to Ireland, 1973.

Neath Boys' Grammar School rugby team, 1940-41.

Ynysygerwn Cricket Club first XI,1955.

Ynysygerwn Cricket Club's South Wales League, championship winning team, 1956.

The netball team at Groes Primary School, Margam, pictured with Mayor of Afan, Councillor Ted Owen at the Mayor's parlour, where they were entertained after a successful season, 1975.

Participants in the Mumbles to Aberavon row, organised by Port Talbot Round Table, 1970s. They are having a wash down after the event.

Briton Ferry Steel Bowls Club members, mid-1960s.

The third year rugby team at Dyffryn Comprehensive School, Port Talbot, 1977. Teacher John Bevan is on the left and deputy headteacher John Argyle, on the right.

Members and officials of BP Llandarcy Rugby Club who embarked on a tour of Norway, May 1972.

Cimla RFC players and officials after winning all of the Neath & District league trophies, 1976.

Neath Boys' Club, under nines football team, February 1981.

Neath Karate Club, mid-1980s.

The gymnastics team of the 2nd Port Talbot Boys' Brigade, 1981.

Harlequin Wanderers AFC, Port Talbot Sunday League Champions, 1975-76.

Members of Port Talbot RAFA club cricket team, winners in the Port Talbot League six-a-side tournament, receive their trophy from the Mayor of Port Talbot, Councillor Graham Jones, 1977.

Tonmawr Rugby Club was the scene of some serious darting during September, 1981 when Welsh international darts star Alan Evans played an exhibition tournament against 14 of the top players from the Neath & District Clubs Charity Darts League.

Visit www.bryngoldbooks.com for other titles available including:

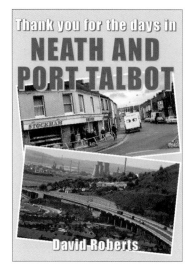

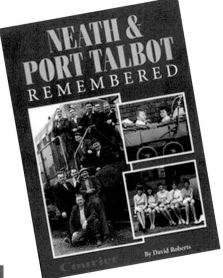

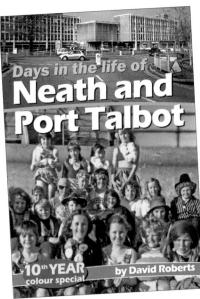

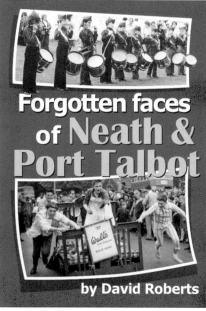

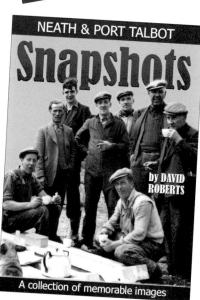

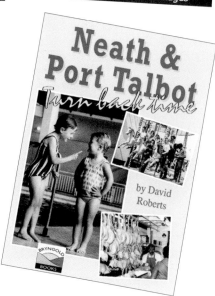

To buy any of these titles tel: 01639 643961 or
email: info@bryngoldbooks.com

www.bryngoldbooks.com